DELICIOUS LOW FAT RECIPES IN 30 MINUTES

Make simple, healthy and satisfying low fat recipes in 30 minutes

Disclaimer

Contents

Introduction

Fat is usually where the flavour in food comes from. Unfortunately excess fat increases the cholesterol level, which in turn increases the risk of heart disease. We have all been told to minimise fat intake for a healthy lifestyle. Most of the people think that low fat diet is tasteless. Eliminating fat from your diet doesn't mean you have to eat foods that are boring or bland.

This book offers a healthy and enjoyable eating plan ready in just 30 minutes that won't deprive you of your favourite foods. From breakfast to dinner, you'll find a comprehensive collection of delicious and imaginative dishes suited for every taste and occasion. Each recipe is accompanied by nutritional information. These recipes have been selected for light and nutritious meals that form the basis of a healthy lifestyle.

There are tempting recipes for appetizers, salads, breakfast, side dishes, light lunches and main courses that cut down on fat but don't compromise on nutrition and taste. These low fat recipes are made with healthy fats like extra virgin olive oil, nuts, lean meat and fish and healthy carbs like brown rice and whole-wheat bread. These recipes will greatly lower your consumption of fat, plus they are easy to make with easy to find ingredients.

There are more than 35 mouth-watering recipes to choose from, with ample vegetarian choices like salad with ranch dressing, pumpkin pasta, potato with butter drizzle, lime quinoa and asparagus pasta. There is variety of recipes with meat too including morrocon style chicken, sausage in herbed tomato sauce, seafood patties, pan seared scallops and duck wraps.

Whether you are on a weight loss diet or simply looking to cook and eat more healthy foods, there are plenty of tasty and filling low fat meal options to explore. Now it is possible to cook delicious, savoury food whilst keeping the fat content to a minimum.

Breakfast

Phyllo Nests with Berries & Yoghurt

Delicious and elegant phyllo nests made with low fat berries and yoghurt

Serves 6

Cooking Time 25 minutes

Nutritional Information: Calories 72 ,Total Fat 1g, Protein 2g, Carbohydrates 14g, Dietary Fiber 2g

Ingredients

1/2 cup raspberries

1/2 cup blueberries

1/2 cup strawberries, halved

6 sheets phyllo dough (14 inches x 9 inches)

Butter-flavored cooking spray

1 teaspoon grated orange peel

1 teaspoon orange juice

2-1/2 teaspoons sugar, divided

1/3 cup vanilla yogurt

Fresh mint leaves

Cooking Method

1. Mix yogurt, orange juice, orange peel and 1 teaspoon of sugar in a small bowl. Refrigerate for a couple of minutes.
2. To avoid phyllo from drying out keep it covered with plastic wrap.
3. Take two sheets of phyllo dough and coat with butter flavoured spray. Place one sheet on the work surface and top it with another sheet of phyllo. Cut the layered phyllo into 6 squares. Repeat with the remaining four phyllo.
4. Coat 6 muffin cups with cooking spray and stack three squares of layered phyllo in the cups. Take special care to avoid corners from overlapping. Sprinkle one-fourth of teaspoon sugar into each cup.
5. Spritz with cooking spray. Place the cups into oven and bake until golden brown fat 375°. Let it cool for a while before serving
6. Now take out the yogurt mixture from refrigerator and spoon into cups. Top with berries and mint leaves

Peach-Berry Compote and Waffles

Best tasting waffles with orange juice and flaxseed served with peach berry compote

Serves 6

Cooking Time 30 minutes

Nutritional Information: Calories 251 ,Total Fat 4g, Protein 7g, Carbohydrates 47g, Dietary Fiber 4g

Ingredients

1 cup blueberries

1/2 cup sliced strawberries

1 cup chopped peaches

2 tablespoons brown sugar

1/4 teaspoon ground cinnamon

1/2 cup orange juice

BATTER:

1/2 cup whole wheat flour

1-1/4 cups all-purpose flour

2 tablespoons flaxseed

1/2 teaspoon ground cinnamon

1 teaspoon baking powder

1 teaspoon baking soda

3/4 cup orange juice

1 cup buttermilk

1 tablespoon canola oil

1 teaspoon vanilla extract

Cooking Method

Compote:

1. Heat a nonstick pan over medium heat.
2. Add in peaches, orange juice, cinnamon and sugar. Bring to a boil. Keep stirring to avoid sticking to the pan
3. Now add the berries. Cook for ten minutes until the mixture thickens.

Waffles:

4. To make great waffles it is always advisable to mix the dry ingredients and wet ingredients separately.
5. Take whole wheat flour and all purpose in a large bowl. Add in flaxseed, baking powder, cinnamon and baking soda to it. Mix everything.
6. Combine the buttermilk, vanilla, orange juice and oil and in a separate bowl.
7. Now add the dry ingredients into the moist ingredients slowly to avoid any lump formation. Mix well.
8. Preheat a waffle iron and bake the bake until golden brown. It yields 12 waffles
9. Serve with compote of berries.

Scrambled Eggs in Pita Pockets

Quick and light pita pockets stuffed with scrambled eggs, green onions, pepper and pimientos

Serves 29

Cooking Time 15 minutes

Nutritional Information: Calories 207 ,Total Fat 6g, Protein 13g, Carbohydrates 28g, Dietary Fiber 4g

Ingredients

3 Eggland's Best Eggs

1 jar (2 ounces) diced pimientos, drained

6 whole wheat pita pocket halves

1 cup fresh or frozen corn

1/4 cup chopped green pepper

1/2 onion

1-1/4 cups egg substitute

1/4 cup fat-free evaporated milk

1/2 teaspoon seasoned salt

1 tablespoon butter

1 medium tomato, seeded and chopped

1 green onion

Cooking Method

1. Chop onion and tomato. Cut green onion and pimientos into slices.
2. Take 1 tablespoon of butter in a large nonstick skillet over medium heat.
3. Add in corn, onion, pimientos and pepper. Sauté for 5-7 minutes until all the vegetables turns tender.
4. Meanwhile whisk eggs in a large bowl with a fork. Add in milk, salt and the egg. Mix everything well with a spatula
5. Now pour this mixture into the skillet.
6. Cover it for a while over medium heat until eggs are completely set.
7. Add in the chopped tomato and green onion over cooked eggs.
8. Take pita and spoon about 2/3 cup of the egg mixture into each half.
9. Serve immediately.

Banana Oatmeal with Brown Sugar & Cinnamon

Banana oatmeal with classic flavors of brown sugar & cinnamon

Serves 3

Cooking time 15 minutes

Nutritional Information: Calories 216 ,Total Fat 2.5g, Protein 10g, Carbohydrates 43g, Dietary Fiber 4g

Ingredients

1 cup quick-cooking oats

2 cups fat-free milk

2 teaspoons brown sugar

1 large ripe banana

1 teaspoon honey

Additional fat-free milk

1/2 teaspoon ground cinnamon

Cooking Method

1. Boil milk in a small saucepan first. Reduce the flame to medium heat.
2. Add in oats and cook for 3-4 minutes until the mixture thickened. Keep stirring to avoid burning.
3. Peel and cut the banana into small slices.
4. Add the banana slices, honey, brown sugar and cinnamon into the milk.
5. Spoon among three serving bowls.
6. If you want you can add extra milk.

Gingered Yoghurt with Fruits & Honey

Festive, delicious fruit yoghurt with a zing of ginger & honey

Serves 4

Cooking time 15 minutes

Nutritional Information: Calories 187 ,Total Fat 2.5g, Protein 13g, Carbohydrates 30g, Dietary Fiber 3.2g

Ingredients

2 cups low-fat Greek yogurt

1 cup quartered strawberries

3 tablespoons sugar

2 teaspoons grated fresh ginger

3 oranges, segmented

2 tsp. honey

1 tablespoon lime juice

Cooking Method

1. Combine strawberries and oranges in a small bowl.
2. Melt sugar with 3 tbsp of water in a medium saucepan over medium heat.
3. Add ginger stripes and lime juice into the sugar syrup.
4. Remove from heat and let it cool for 2-3 minutes.
5. Pour this lukewarm syrup over strawberries and oranges.
6. Spoon yogurt in four bowls.
7. Drizzle each with 1/2 tsp. honey.
8. Add fruit mixture over yogurt.

Spinach and Radish Salad with Ranch Dressing

A light, tasty and colorful radish and spinach salad with ranch dressing

Serves 3

Cooking time 10 minutes

Nutritional Information: Calories 103, Total Fat 3g, Protein 5.6g, Carbohydrates 20.5g, Dietary Fiber 6g

Ingredients

1 cup plain low fat yogurt

2 tablespoons grated red onion

1 cup shredded carrots

1 cup shredded radish

3 cups fresh baby spinach

2 tablespoons chopped dill

2 tablespoons chopped parsley leaves

1 tablespoon lemon juice

1 clove garlic

Black pepper

Sea Salt

Cooking Method

1. Take carrots and radishes in a bowl and mix it with the spinach leaves.
2. Whisk low fat yogurt in another bowl
3. Add grated onion, lemon juice, parsley and dill to it.
4. Add a generous pinch of salt into the chopped garlic and mash with the side of a spoon or knife.
5. Mix this paste into the yoghurt dressing.
6. Pour the dressing over the salad.
7. Toss and sprinkle some freshly grounded black pepper on it.
8. Refrigerate it for a couple of minutes before serving.

Low Fat Tuna Salad Sandwich

A traditional, classic tuna fish sandwich recipe with different textures

Serves 4

Cooking time 15 minutes

Nutritional Information: Calories 246, Total Fat 4g, Protein 18g, Carbohydrates 33g, Dietary Fiber 5.2 g

Ingredients

1 7-ounce vacuum packed tuna

1/3 cup fat-free mayonnaise

8 slices whole grain bread

1/2 cup pre-shredded coleslaw mix

1/4 cup finely chopped onion

1 tsp cider vinegar

Romaine lettuce leaves

1 tomato, sliced

Salt to taste

Freshly ground black pepper

Cooking Method

1. Toast the slices of whole grain bread in a toaster
2. To make sandwich filling; combine tuna, mayonnaise and coleslaw mix in large bowl
3. Add in cider vinegar and onion to the tuna.
4. Sprinkle with salt and black pepper as per your taste
5. Line one side of toasted bread with lettuce leaves. Place tuna salad over it.
6. Garnish with tomato slices.
7. Add another lettuce leaf and a piece of bread.
8. Make four sandwiches and serve.

Quinoa Risotto with Mushroom and Asparagus

A quick crunchy risotto recipe made with quinoa, asparagus and parmesan

Serves 4

Cooking time 25 minutes

Nutritional Information: Calories 301, Total Fat 7g, Protein 13g, Carbohydrates 52g, Dietary Fiber 3g

Ingredients

350g chestnut mushrooms, sliced

175g arborio rice

1 cup chopped fresh asparagus spears

100g quinoa

6-7 cups hot vegetable stock

1/2 cup grated parmesan

1/2 cup thyme leaves

Rocket leaves to serve

Salt & Pepper to taste

1 tbsp olive oil

Cooking Method

1. Heat oil in a large stock pot, sauté the mushrooms for 2-3 minutes until tender and releasing juice.
2. Keep the stock in separate pan on a low heat.
3. Add quinoa to the mushrooms.
4. Add a ladle of the stock and stir until absorbed.
5. Stir in the rice, asparagus and the remaining stock. Bring to a simmer until all the stock has been used up.
6. When rice and quinoa are tender and cooked stir in the thyme leaves.
7. Season, to taste, with salt and black pepper.
8. Top with grated Parmesan and rocket leaves.
9. Ladle risotto into bowls and serve hot.

Tofu & Soy Quiches with Mushrooms

Super quick & super tasty mini vegetable-and-egg casseroles with tofu and soy cheese

Serves 5

Cooking time 30 minutes

Nutritional Information: Calories 108 , Total Fat 6g, Protein10 g, Carbohydrates 5g, Dietary Fiber1 g

Ingredients

1 1/2 cups button mushrooms

1 12 1/4 ounce package light firm silken-style tofu

12 ounces fresh asparagus spears

1/2 cup refrigerated or frozen egg product, thawed

3/4 cup finely shredded cheddar-flavored soy cheese

2 tablespoons snipped fresh basil

1/4 teaspoon ground black pepper

2 teaspoons olive oil

1/4 cup chopped shallots

1/8 teaspoon salt

15x10x1 inch baking pan

Six 6-ounce ramekins

Cooking Method

1. Preheat oven to 350° F
2. Trim asparagus ends and cut into 1-inch long pieces.
3. Cut mushrooms into slices. Likewise chop the shallots finely.
4. Blend tofu and eggs in a blender or food processor
5. Transfer the tofu mixture to a large bowl; add in soy cheese, pepper, 1 tablespoon of the basil, and salt. Mix well and keep it aside.
6. In a nonstick pan, heat oil over medium-high heat.
7. Add asparagus mushrooms and shallots to it.
8. Cover and let it simmer for 8-9 minutes.
9. When the vegetables turn tender remove from heat and let it cool.
10. Combine this mushroom & asparagus mixture into tofu mixture. Mix with a spatula.
11. Divide this mixture among six ramekins.
12. Place these ramekins in a baking pan.
13. Bake, uncovered, for 18-20 minutes until set
14. Garnish with basil and serve.

Leek, Mushroom & Cheese Pancakes

A delicious pancake with a filling of leek, cheese & mushrooms especially for sunday's breakfast

Serves 4

Cooking time 30 minutes

Nutritional Information: Calories 201, Total Fat 3 g, Protein 19g, Carbohydrates 27g, Dietary Fiber 2g

Ingredients

100g flour

1 pinch salt

1 medium egg

300ml skimmed milk

1 spray low-fat cooking spray

1 portion leek

100g mushrooms, sliced

1 stock cube

20g butter

40g flour

300ml skimmed milk

50g half-fat cheddar cheese, grated

1tbsp parsley, or

1tsp fresh chives

Cooking Method

1. To make the pancake batter, whisk egg and milk together in a mixing bowl.
2. Add in salt and flour into the bowl. Make a smooth batter by beating together everything.
3. Heat a large nonstick pan and coat evenly with low-fat cooking spray.
4. To make pancakes add 1/4 of the batter and swirl it around the pan.
5. When the surface is set flip it over with a spatula to cook the other side.
6. Make all the four pancakes and keep in a warm place.
7. In a saucepan fry the leek until soft then add mushroom and vegetable stock and cook till cooked. Drain well, reserving the stock.
8. Take butter in a non-stick saucepan over medium heat.
9. When it's all melted; add the flour and reserved stock and cook for 5 minutes stirring continuously until smooth and thickened.
10. Add in grated cheese and.
11. Add the leek, mushrooms and herbs and let simmer for 2-3 minutes. This will be used as a filling for the pancakes
12. Finish off the pancakes with the mushroom & leek filling and serve.

Farro-Smothered Creamy Mushrooms

Delightful farro- smothered portobello in a creamy sauce

Serves 6

Cooking time 30 minutes

Nutritional Information: Calories 215, Total Fat 6g, Protein 12g, Carbohydrates 28g, Dietary Fiber 3g

Ingredients

65 inch fresh portobello mushrooms

1/4 cup snipped dried tomatoes

1cup semi-pearled farro

Nonstick cooking spray

1/2 teaspoon dried thyme, crushed

4ounces soft goat cheese, cut up

1/4cup finely shredded Parmesan cheese

1/4cup sliced green onion tops

2 cups coarsely chopped fresh Swiss chard leaves

3 cups reduced-sodium vegetable broth

Freshly ground black pepper

Cooking Method

1. Clean the portobello mushrooms and remove its stems and gills.
2. Preheat a grill pan over medium heat.
3. Add vegetable broth in a skillet and bring it to a boil.
4. When it just starts boiling; add in farro. Cover it and let simmer 10-15 minutes.
5. Coat both sides of mushrooms with cooking spray.
6. Add mushrooms to the grill pan. Cook both sides of the mushrooms for 7-10 minutes or until tender.
7. To the farro add swiss chard, thyme and dried tomatoes
8. Cover and cook until farro is tender. Turn off the heat. Add in goat cheese and let it melt.
9. Take a serving platter and place mushrooms on it with stemmed sides up.
10. Spoon farro mixture over mushrooms. Garnish with Parmesan cheese, green onion and pepper.

Baked Souffléd potatoes

Serves 4

Cooking time 30 minutes

Nutritional Information: Calories 219, Total Fat 3.6g, Protein 23g, Carbohydrates 41g, Dietary Fiber 2.3g

Ingredients

125g (4 oz) ham, chopped

675g (1 1/2lbs) potatoes, peeled and cut into chunks

2 medium eggs

150 ml (1/4pt)) milk

30ml (1 oz) tomato relish

Cooking Method

1. Pre-heat oven to 220°C/425°F/gas 7.
2. Bring salted water to a boil and add potatoes in it. Cook for 15 minutes until potatoes are tender. Drain the potatoes when cooked.
3. Boil milk in a separate pan. Let it cool and then pour over the potato with some pepper and salt. Mash all the ingredients together until smooth.

4. Separate the egg yolk from egg whites.
5. Add the tomato relish, yolks and ham to the potato.
6. Mix everything together.
7. Whisk the egg whites until stiff then using a tablespoon fold the egg whites into the potato mixture.
8. Spoon the mixture into 4, lightly greased ramekin dishes. Bake for 15 minutes.
9. Serve your souffléd potatoes immediately.

Lunch

Penne with Broccoli, Sausages and Ricotta

A recipe for penne including broccoli rabe, turkey sausages and ricotta

Serves 6

Cooking time 25 minutes

Nutritional Information: Calories 342 ,Total Fat 8g, Protein 18g, Carbohydrates 47g, Dietary Fiber 2g

Ingredients

12 ounces whole wheat penne

1 bunch broccoli rabe

1/4 cup part-skim ricotta

1/2 medium red onion, thinly sliced

1 garlic clove, sliced

1 tablespoon extra virgin olive oil

Small pinch crushed red pepper flakes

2 tablespoons tomato paste

2 lean Italian turkey sausages, casings removed

2 tablespoons grated Parmesan

Salt to taste

Cooking Method

1. Fill a large skillet with salted water and bring to a boil.
2. Add in the broccoli rabe; cover and let simmer for 6 minutes until tender
3. Remove from heat and let it cool.
4. Chop the broccoli into bite-size pieces in a colander.
5. Cook penne according to the package directions until al dente. Drain and reserve 1/2 cup of the pasta water.
6. Take another large skillet over medium heat and add some olive oil.
7. Add in onion and garlic; sauté for 5 minutes. Stir sausages and red pepper flakes and cook for 10 minutes until browned crumbling the sausage with a spoon.
8. Add in chopped broccoli and sauté for about 3 more minutes.
9. Add in tomato paste to sausage and broccoli. Mix everything with a wooden spoon and cook for another 2 minutes.
10. Add in pasta along with pasta water. Adjust the heat to low.
11. Toss to combine the ingredients.
12. Finish the dish off with ricotta and Parmesan. Serve immediately.

Turkey & Black Bean stuffed Chimichangas

Easy & quick chimchangas stuffed with black beans, salsa and turkey

Serves 6

Cooking time 30 minutes

Nutritional Information: Calories 206, Total Fat 4g, Protein 23g, Carbohydrates 33g, Dietary Fiber 18 g

Ingredients

610 inches whole wheat flour tortillas

1-3/4 cup cooked black beans

8 ounces uncooked ground turkey breast

114 1/2 ounce can no-salt-added diced tomatoes, drained

1/4cup bottled salsa

1/2cup chopped onion

1/4cup snipped fresh cilantro

1tablespoon lime juice

1/2teaspoon ground cumin

1/2cup shredded reduced-fat Monterey Jack cheese

Light dairy sour cream

Fresh cilantro sprigs

Nonstick cooking spray

Cooking Method

1. Coat a baking sheet with nonstick cooking spray. Preheat oven to 425°F.;
2. Wrap the tortillas in foil and heat in the oven for a couple of minutes.
3. Place a large skillet over medium heat coated with cooking spray.
4. Add onion to it and sauté for 2-3 minutes.
5. Add in turkey and cook until turkey is no longer pink
6. Mash black beans gently with your hand and add it to the skillet.
7. Stir in tomato and cook until tender. Add in salsa, 1/4 cup cilantro, cumin and lime juice.
8. Spoon about 1/2 cup of the turkey filling on the center each tortilla. Roll up from the bottom.
9. Secure rolled tortillas with wooden toothpicks.
10. Place wrapped tortillas on baking sheet. C
11. oat top and sides of the filled tortillas with nonstick cooking spray.
12. Bake tortillas until golden brown for 12 minutes.
13. Sprinkle chimichangas with sour cream, cheese and cilantro sprigs.

Grilled Fillets with Basil Tomato Sauce

Tender and flaky halibut fillets seasoned with tomato salsa including orange peels and basil

Serves 2

Cooking time 25 minutes

Nutritional Information: Calories 203, Total Fat 5g, Protein 36g, Carbohydrates 2g

Ingredients

2 halibut fillets (6 ounces each)

1/4 cup diced seeded tomato

1 tablespoon lemon juice

1 tablespoon chopped green onion

1/2 teaspoon dried rosemary, crushed

1-1/2 teaspoons olive oil

1/4 teaspoon salt

Dash pepper

1-1/2 teaspoons red wine vinegar

1 tablespoon minced fresh basil

1/4 teaspoon grated orange peel

Cooking Method

1. Take a large zip plastic bag and put rosemary, lemon juice, oil, pepper and salt; mix well.
2. Add in fish fillets. Coat the fillets with the herbs mixture in the bag and refrigerate.
3. Coat the grill rack with a paper towel moistened with cooking spray.
4. Grill halibut for a couple of minutes. Use long-handled tongs to turn the fillets.
5. To make sauce cook tomato with green onion in a small saucepan over medium heat.
6. When tomato is cooked through, add in orange peel, basil and vinegar with little salt.
7. Remove the sauce from heat and serve with gravy

Duck wraps in Hoisin Sauce

A nice lighter recipe of hoisin duck wraps full of oriental flavor

Serves 2

Cooking time 20 minutes

Nutritional Information: Calories 355, Total Fat 7g, Protein 17g, Carbohydrates 22g, Dietary Fiber 5g

Ingredients

2 flour tortilla wraps

2tbsp hoisin sauce

2tsp sunflower oil

1 red pepper, deseeded and sliced

1/2 cucumber, cut into strips

4-6 spring onion, cut into thin strips

175g pack mini duck fillets

1 Little Gem lettuce, shredded

Sliced spring onion, to serve

Cooking Method

1. Heat sunflower oil in a nonstick pan over medium high heat. Add red peppers and sauté until they are soft.
2. Stir in duck fillets into the peppers and cook for 8-10 minutes until the duck is cooked through. Remove from heat.
3. Let it cool for 2-3 minutes than add hoisin sauce to fillets.
4. To make the wraps; place cucumber, lettuce and spring onion on a tortilla wrap.
5. Spoon the red pepper and duck mixture on it and top with spring onion
6. Roll up and cut each wraps into two halves.
7. Serve with extra hoisin sauce and cucumber strips.

Artichoke and Tomato pizza

Healthy yet tasty tomato pizza topped with artichoke, roasted peppers & olives

Serves 4

Cooking time 20 minutes

Nutritional Information: Calories 301, Total Fat 8g, Protein 34g, Carbohydrates 27g, Dietary Fiber 1.2g

Ingredients

390g can artichoke hearts in brine, drained

4 flour tortillas

4tbsp tomato ketchup

6 baby plum tomatoes, halved

2 red onions, peeled and thinly sliced

2-3 flame-roasted peppers, sliced

12 black olives

125g ready-grated mozzarella

Freshly ground black pepper

Cooking Method

1. Set the grill to medium/ high.
2. Place the tortillas on two baking sheets.
3. Spread tomato ketchup on the tortillas,
4. Top with the roasted peppers and onion slices,
5. Add halved artichokes, olives and baby plum tomatoes.
6. Sprinkle with the grated mozzarella cheese.
7. Place two tortillas on the grill at a time and grill for 7 minutes, until the cheese melts.
8. Keep an eye on the tortillas and don't let them go too brown
9. Season with freshly ground black pepper.
10. Roll up and serve straightaway with your favorite salad.

Fried Honey Beef with Bok Choy

Stir fried pieces of beef, bok choy and broccoli tossed in a soy sauce and money mixture

Serves 4

Cooking time 30 minutes

Nutritional Information: Calories 450 , Total Fat 7.6g, Protein 35g, Carbohydrates 57g, Dietary Fiber 5g

Ingredients

500g rump steak, thinly sliced

1 teaspoon Chinese five Spice

2 tablespoons Chinese rice wine (or dry sherry)

1 tablespoon reduced-salt soy sauce

1 tablespoon honey

Cooking oil spray

1 white onion, cut into thin wedges

1 bunch Chinese broccoli

1 red capsicum, seeded, thinly sliced

1 bunch baby bok choy

Cooking Method

1. Cut broccoli with its stems into 5 cm long pieces. Trim bok choy and separate the leaves.
2. Coat steak gently with Chinese five spices.
3. Combine rice wine, soy sauce and honey in a separate bowl.
4. Place a large skillet over high heat coated with cooking spray.
5. Add in the steaks and fry for 3 minutes until browned.
6. Stir-fry all steaks in batches .Remove from heat and set aside to rest.
7. Return skillet to high heat and spray some more oil.
8. Add onion wedges and sauté for 3 minutes.
9. Add in broccoli stems and sauté for 2 minute.
10. Add baby bok choy, broccoli leaves, capsicum and a little water. Cook everything for 5 minutes, until vegetables are tender-crisp.
11. Return beef to skillet and add wine, soy sauce and honey mixture.
12. Toss until well combined. Serve immediately.

Soba Noodles with Salmon in Mirin Sauce

Amazing combination of noodles, salmon and asparagus with a dressing of mirin, soy sauce and sesame oil

Serves 4

Cooking time 20 minutes

Nutritional Information: Calories 287 , Total Fat 6g, Protein 19g, Carbohydrates 40g, Dietary Fiber 1g

Ingredients

150g salmon fillet

200g dried soba noodles

1 bunch asparagus, trimmed, sliced diagonally

2 teaspoons sesame oil

75g baby spinach leaves

2 tablespoons mirin (Japanese rice wine)

1 tablespoon lime juice

1 tablespoon salt-reduced soy sauce

1 Lebanese cucumber

2 teaspoons sesame seeds, lightly toasted

Cooking Method
1. Take cucumber; trim and make thin slices.
2. Salmon should hot smoked with sweet chilli. Remove the skin.
3. Bring water to a boil in a large saucepan. Add soba noodles and 2 drops of sesame oil and cook according to packet instructions.
4. Rinse under cold running water. Keep it aside to cool.
5. Blanch asparagus in boiling water for a couple of minutes. It will turn bright green.
6. Rinse asparagus too under cold running water.
7. For the dressing: combine mirin, soy sauce, lime juice and remaining sesame oil in a small bowl.
8. Place noodles, salmon, asparagus, spinach, cucumber and dressing into a large bowl. Toss to combine the ingredients
9. Serve noodles on serving plates. Sprinkle with toasted sesame seeds.

Seafood Patties with Chili Dipping Sauce

Mouth watering patties made of fish & prawns and served with chilli dipping sauce

Serves 4

Cooking time 30 minutes

Nutritional Information: Calories 213, Total Fat 3g, Protein34 g, Carbohydrates 6g, Dietary Fiber 1g

Ingredients

300g firm white fish fillets, chopped

300g uncooked medium prawns

1/4 bunch coriander, stalks and leaves chopped

2 large garlic cloves, crushed

3 green onions, trimmed, chopped

2 egg whites cooking oil spray

1/2 cup mirin

1/2 cup salt-reduced soy sauce

Dipping sauce

1 red birdseye chilli, finely chopped

Patties

Cooking Method

1. Combine the prawns, fish, garlic, onion, coriander, and egg whites in a food processor and process.
2. Take this mixture out and divide into 16 portions. Make 16 patties with each portion.
3. Line a baking tray with baking paper.
4. Place the patties on baking tray. Cover with plastic wrap and refrigerate for 15 minutes.
5. To make dipping sauce; combine soy sauce, mirin and chilli in a small bowl.
6. Spray patties all over with cooking oil.
7. Heat a large non-stick frying pan over medium-high heat.
8. Place patties to pan and cook for a couple of minutes until golden brown. Turn and cook the other side.
9. Cook all the patties in batches
10. Transfer to a serving platter. Serve fish patties warm with dipping sauce.

Shrimp à la Grecque with Marjoram

Shrimp cooked in white wine and feta cheese having flavors of the mediterranean

Serves 4

Cooking time 27 minutes

Nutritional Information: Calories 279, Total Fat 10g, Protein 32g, Carbohydrates 5.6g, Dietary Fiber 2g

Ingredients

1 1/2 pounds large shrimp

2 cups chopped canned tomatoes, drained

1/2 cup dry white wine

1 tablespoon minced garlic

2 tablespoons finely chopped parsley

1/2 teaspoon dried marjoram, crushed

1/4 teaspoon salt

1/4 teaspoon black pepper

3 ounces feta cheese, cut into 1/2-inch cubes

2 tablespoons extra virgin olive oil

Cooking Method

1. Peel and devein the shrimp and sprinkle with salt and pepper.
2. Heat oil in a saucepan over medium heat.
3. Add garlic and sauté for 1 minute.
4. Add tomatoes, 1 tablespoon parsley, white wine and marjoram.
5. Season with salt and pepper.
6. Cook over medium-high heat until sauce thickens.
7. Add shrimp into the saucepan and cook for about 6-7 minutes until shrimp turn pink.
8. Add cheese to the shrimps. Keep stirring gently. Take special care to avoid cheese from crumbling.
9. Garnish with remaining parsley. Serve hot over orzo.

Potato with Orange Essence and Butter Drizzle

A delicious mash of sweet potatoes with an essence of orange is great for brightening up your plate

Serves 2

Cooking time 17 minutes

Nutritional Information: Calories 334, Total Fat 6g, Protein 5g, Carbohydrates 67g, Dietary Fiber 6g

Ingredients

4 sweet potatoes, peeled and cut into a large dice

1 tsp olive oil

1 tbsp unsalted butter

1 tbsp orange juice

4 small sage leaves

Orange zest (pinch)

1/2 teaspoon salt

1/4 teaspoon ground nutmeg

Cooking Method

1. Steam sweet potatoes in salted water in a saucepan over medium heat.
2. Cook the potatoes until they are tender for 15 minutes. Reserve about 1/4 cup of cooking water for later use
3. Drain in a colander and mash the potatoes along with the reserved cooking water
4. Mix olive oil, orange juice, zest, nutmeg and salt into the mash.
5. Spoon the potato mash into a serving dish.
6. In a small saucepan, melt the butter until browned over medium heat.
7. Reduce the heat and add in sage leaves immediately.
8. When it starts foaming and bubbling remove it.
9. Pour the sage butter directly over potato mash and serve immediately.

Spicy Pork Tenderloin with Seasoned Rub

A richly flavoured summertime meal of juicy pork tenderloin with an aromatic spice mixture

Serves 4

Cooking time 30 minutes

Nutritional Information: Calories 211, Total Fat 9.5g, Protein 31g, Carbohydrates 2g, Dietary Fiber 1g

Ingredients

1 1/4 pounds pork tenderloin

1 teaspoon dried thyme

1 teaspoon dried oregano

1 teaspoon garlic powder

1 teaspoon ground cumin

1 teaspoon ground coriander

1 tablespoon olive oil

1 teaspoon minced garlic

Salt

Cooking Method

1. Preheat the oven to 450 degrees F.
2. Combine all the dry ingredients such as coriander, garlic powder, cumin, thyme, oregano, and salt in a bowl. This will be used as a rub for the pork.
3. Sprinkle the rub over the tenderloin with a dry hand.
4. Press meat gently into the rub so that the seasoning adheres well to the tenderloin.
5. Add olive oil in a large skillet over medium-high heat.
6. Add in minced garlic and sauté for 30 seconds.
7. Add in pork tenderloin in the pan and cook for about 8 minutes.
8. Use tongs to turn the meat to ensure both sides are cooked.
9. Transfer tenderloin to a roasting pan in the preheated oven and bake for 22 minutes.
10. Cut into slices and serve.

Dinner

Chicken Fricassee with White Wine and Vegetables

An instant and classic stew with chicken breasts simmering in white wine is sure to bring you comfort

Serves 4

Cooking time 30 minutes

Nutritional Information: Calories 252, Total Fat 5g, Protein 30.5g, Carbohydrates 19.5g, Dietary Fiber 3g

Ingredients

4 (6-ounce) skinned chicken breast halves

1/4 cup dry white wine

3 tablespoons all-purpose flour

2 cups (3-inch) julienne-cut carrot

1 teaspoon paprika

1 teaspoon poultry seasoning

1/2 teaspoon freshly ground black pepper

2 teaspoons butter

1 1/2 cups chopped onion

1/2 cup chopped celery

1 cup fat-free, lower-sodium chicken broth

3 garlic cloves, minced

1/4 cup chopped fresh parsley

1/2 teaspoon salt

Cooking Method

1. Combine flour, paprika, poultry seasoning, salt and pepper in a large zip-closed plastic bag.
2. Add chicken breast into the bag; toss well.
3. Coat the chicken with the flour mixture, then remove chicken pieces from bag and reserve flour mixture.
4. Take one tablespoon of butter in a large non-stick pan over medium heat.
5. Add chicken with the breast sides down; sauté for 5 minutes.
6. When chicken looks golden brown remove it from pan
7. Add garlic and sauté for 1 minute.
8. Add in onion and celery to pan; sauté for 6 more minutes.
9. Add the remaining reserved flour mixture and stir for 1 minute.
10. Add white wine and broth; bring to a boil. Add carrot.
11. Return chicken to pan. This time keep the breast sides up.
12. Cover it with a lid and let it simmer for 20 minutes. Garnish with the chopped parsley.

Pan-Seared Scallops over Rice Salad

Perfect pan seared scallops served with rice salad including beans, corn and jalapenos

Serves 4

Cooking time minutes

Nutritional Information: Calories 420 , Total Fat 5g, Protein 29g, Carbohydrates 63g, Dietary Fiber 8g

Ingredients

16 dry scallops

3 cups cooked brown rice

1/2 cup chopped scallions

1 lime

2 teaspoons olive oil

1 can corn, drained

1 teaspoon chili powder

1/2 teaspoon salt

1 cup grape tomatoes, halved

1/2 cup jalapenos

1 can black beans, rinsed and drained

2 tablespoons chopped fresh cilantro

Cooking Method

1. Combine half lime juice, 1 teaspoon olive oil in a large bowl.
2. Add in1/2 teaspoon chili powder and salt. Mix well.
3. Add scallions, beans, tomatoes, corn, jalapenos and cilantro.
4. Toss gently to combine everything.
5. Stir in cooked rice, and toss until thoroughly combined.
6. Pat scallops dry with a paper towel.
7. Mix 1 teaspoon olive oil, 1/2 teaspoon chili powder and salt in a large bowl. Toss scallops in this oil mixture.
8. Now squeeze juice from remaining half lime into it and set aside.
9. Heat a large nonstick skillet over medium-high heat.
10. Arrange all scallops in the skillet with flat sides down.
11. Cook each side for 3-4 minutes until lightly browned and opaque in the center.
12. Pour lime juice over scallops and toss gently.
13. Divide salad into 4 servings and top with scallops.

Baked Pumpkin Pasta

Perfect for fall, this delicious baked pumpkin pasta makes a great weeknight meal on cold evenings

Serves 6

Cooking time 30 minutes

Nutritional Information: Calories 349, Total Fat 5g, Protein 15.9g, Carbohydrates 54g, Dietary Fiber 5.2g

Ingredients

1 15 ounce can pure pumpkin

2 small zucchini, halved & sliced

12 ounces uncooked penne pasta

2 tsp olive oil

1 medium onion, finely chopped

1 tsp dried sage

2 cloves garlic, finely chopped

1 teaspoon red pepper flakes

1/2 tsp dried thyme

1 cup fat free ricotta cheese

1/2 cup shredded parmesan cheese

1/2 cup water reserved from pasta pot

Cooking Method

1. Preheat oven to 400 degrees
2. Cook pasta. Remove 3 minutes before it is fully cooked.
3. Meanwhile heat oil in large saucepan.
4. Add in onions and garlic and crushed red pepper flakes to the saucepan and sauté, stirring occasionally until soft, about 2 minutes.
5. Stir in sliced zucchini, sage, thyme and salt. Sauté for 5 minutes.
6. Stir in canned pumpkin and ricotta cheese. Lower the heat and let simmer for a couple of minutes.
7. Mix drained pasta and 1/2 cup of reserved pasta water into the saucepan and mix well.
8. Spoon pasta into 11 x 7 baking dish. Top with cheese. Bake for 10 minutes.

BBQ Steaks with Ketchup Sauce and Smoky Corn

Absolutely delicious pork steaks made in a ketchup sauce and served with smoky corn

Serves 4

Cooking time 20 minutes

Nutritional Information: Calories 310, Total Fat 9g, Protein 32g, Carbohydrates 33g, Dietary Fiber 2g

Ingredients

4 corn on the cobs

4 pork loin steaks, trimmed of any fat

2 tbsp dark muscovado sugar

1 tbsp white wine vinegar

1 tsp paprika

4 tsp tomato ketchup

1 tbsp butter

Cooking Method

1. Boil water in a pan for the corn. Put the corn into the boiling water and cook until tender. Drain the corn and keep aside
2. To make the sauce by mixing half of the paprika, ketchup, vinegar and muscovado sugar.
3. Heat a non-stick barbeque pan, and brown the pork for a couple of minutes on each side.
4. Spoon over the sauce when halfway done and turn the steaks in it until the pork is cooked through and sticky.
5. Take some butter in a heatproof bowl and add the remaining paprika into it.
6. Microwave on High for 20 seconds until the paprika is sizzling in the melted butter
7. Brush this smoky butter over the corn.
8. Serve with the sticky pork steaks and green salad.

Ground Turkey Pilaf with Nutmeg & Apricot

A healthy combination of dried fruit with ground turkey and wild rice

Serves 4

Cooking time 25 minutes

Nutritional Information: Calories 215, Total Fat 5g, Protein 27g, Carbohydrates 37g

Ingredients

1/2 lb. ground Turkey

1/2 cup chopped dried apricots

1 tbsp. Canola oil

1/4 cup chopped green onions

1/2 cup dried cherries

1/8 tsp. ground nutmeg

6 oz. pkg. quick cooking long grain and wild rice mix

2 cups vegetable stock

Cooking Method

1. Heat canola oil in large saucepan over medium heat; add green onions and sauté for 1 minute
2. Add turkey, crumble and cook until turkey turns tender and is no longer pink. About 6-8 minutes.
3. Stir in wild rice and seasoning packet from rice mix.
4. Add vegetable stock and bring to a boil, stirring occasionally; reduce heat to low.
5. Add in apricots, nutmeg and cherries.
6. Cover and simmer for 15-16 minutes until rice is tender and dry fruits are heated through.

Italian Sausage with Beans in Tomato Sauce

A hearty yet low-fat sausage made in herbed tomato sauce that works beautifully over linguine

Serves 6

Cooking time 35 minutes

Nutritional Information: Calories 201, Total Fat 3g, Protein 16g, Carbohydrates 30g, Dietary Fiber 8g

Ingredients

6 ounces sweet Italian chicken sausage, sliced

1 medium onion, chopped

4 ounces mushrooms, sliced

2 cloves garlic, minced

1 stalk celery, thinly sliced

2 14.5-ounce cans diced tomatoes

1 tsp dried oregano

1 16 ounce can cannellini beans

2 tbsp tomato paste

Red pepper flakes

Salt

Freshly ground black pepper

Cooking Method

1. Pick over the beans, discarding any misshapen beans. Rinse the beans and drain.
2. Heat a nonstick skillet coated with cooking spray on medium heat.
3. Add chopped onion, mushrooms garlic, oregano and celery. Sauté for 5 minutes.
4. Add beans, tomatoes and tomato paste, let simmer for 10 minutes Taste and adjust the seasonings with salt and pepper.
5. Heat olive oil in a heavy frying pan over medium-high heat. Place the sausage and cook for 8 to 10 minutes until browned. Turn the sausage over and cook the other side. Drain excess fat.
6. Transfer the sausage to a cutting board; let rest for 3 minutes.
7. Cut the sausages into serving pieces and serve with the cannellini beans and linguine.

Moroccan Style Stewed Chicken

Mouthwatering stewed chicken in moroccan style made with a perfect blend of savory spices

Serves 4

Cooking time 26minutes

Nutritional Information: Calories 352, Total Fat 10g, Protein 28g, Carbohydrates 31g, Dietary Fiber 5g

Ingredients

1 lb chicken thighs (boneless, skinless)

1 cup chicken stock or water

1 can (16 oz) garbanzo beans

1 can (14.5 oz) diced tomatoes

1 large zucchini, cut into cubes

Chopped fresh cilantro

1 tsp ground cumin

1/2 tsp cayenne pepper

1/2 tsp ground cinnamon

1/2 tbsp olive oil

1/4cup slivered almonds, toasted

Salt and pepper to taste

Cooking Method

1. Marinate the chicken thighs with salt and pepper.
2. Heat the oil in a large sauce pan over medium high heat.
3. Add in chicken and cook for 2 to 3 minutes on both sides. Add the zucchini and continue cooking until browned
4. Add the tomatoes, garbanzo beans, chicken stock, cayenne, cinnamon and cumin.
5. Turn the heat to low; cover and let it simmer for 15 minutes, until the chicken is thoroughly cooked.
6. Season taste with salt and pepper and serve with couscous (optional).
7. Garnish with almonds and chopped cilantro.

Lime Quinoa with Cilantro, Spinach and Tomatoes

A quick and easy quinoa salad made with spinach, cilantro and cherry tomatoes

Serves 6

Cooking time 30 minutes

Nutritional Information: Calories 113, Total Fat 3g, Protein 4.8g, Carbohydrates 21.6g, Dietary Fiber 1.6g

Ingredients

1 cup quinoa

2 cups vegetable broth

1/4 cup fresh lemon juice

1 cup spinach

1/2 cup fresh cilantro

1/4 cup onion

1-2 cloves garlic

1/2 cup cherry tomatoes, halved

1 tbsp Dijon mustard

Salt & Pepper to taste

Cooking Method

1. Rinse the quinoa to remove its bitter protective coating.
2. Soak the quinoa in a pot in the vegetable broth for about 10 minutes.
3. Turn the heat on to medium-high and let the quinoa come to a boil.
4. Once it boils reduce the heat to medium-low and let the quinoa simmer.
5. Cook quinoa for next 20 minutes. When cooked keep it aside and let it cool
6. Put spinach and cilantro in a food processor and process until finely diced.
7. Dice onion and garlic in the processor too
8. Add spinach, cilantro, garlic and onion into a bowl and mix well
9. All in cooled quinoa along with tomato into the bowl. Make a dressing of lemon juice, dijon mustard, salt & pepper and pour this over quinoa salad.
10. Let cool in fridge for 5-10 minutes before serving.

Roasted Pork with couscous & Ginger Yogurt

A low-fat yet satisfying pork recipe served with ginger yoghurt sauce is sure to give your metabolism system a boost

Serves 6

Cooking time 30 minutes

Nutritional Information: Calories 279, Total Fat 6g, Protein 22g, Carbohydrates 38g

Ingredients

2 pork fillets, trimmed of any fat

200g fat-free natural yogurt

250g couscous

2 tsp olive oil

3 tsp ground cumin

1 tsp ground cinnamon

100g sultanas

Lemon zest & 1lemon juice

4 tsp grated ginger

1/2 cup chopped mint

Cooking Method

1. Preheat oven to 190C/170C fan/gas 5.
2. Brown the pork in a non-stick frying pan over high heat for a couple of minutes, turning twice.
3. Combine oil, cinnamon, 2 tsp cumin, 2 tsp ginger and some seasoning in a bowl. Rub this mixture all over the pork.
4. Transfer the meat to a roasting tin and roast for 25 minutes. Pierce the pork with a skewer to check if it is thoroughly cooked.
5. Combine the remaining cumin, lemon zest and juice, the sultanas and mix with the couscous. Season and pour this mixture into 400ml boiling water.
6. Add in chopped mint and, stir well and cover for 5 minutes
7. Add in the remaining ginger into the yogurt with a little seasoning
8. Thickly slice the pork and serve with the couscous and ginger yogurt.

Pasta with Asparagus and Cherry Tomatoes

A delightful spring supper made with crisp bright green asparagus, sweet red cherry tomatoes and tossed with farfalle pasta

Serves 6

Cooking time 10 minutes

Nutritional Information: Calories 280, Total Fat 5g, Protein 10g, Carbohydrates 48g, Dietary Fiber 4.2g

Ingredients

12 ounces farfalle (bow tie) pasta

1 pound of medium asparagus spears

1 tbsp olive oil

1/4 cup minced shallots

1 pint cherry tomatoes, halved

2 garlic cloves, crushed

1/4 cup fresh basil, finely chopped

Freshly ground black pepper

2 tbsp balsamic vinegar

1/4 cup freshly grated parmesan cheese

Cooking Method

1. Chop asparagus into 1 1/2-inch pieces. Cook pasta according to directions on package. Drain and reserve the liquid.
2. Heat oil in a large skillet over a medium-high heat.
3. Add shallots and garlic and sauté for a couple of minutes.
4. Add tomatoes, asparagus pieces and sauté until very soft for about 5 minutes.
5. Pour balsamic vinegar and mix well.
6. Add basil and sprinkle freshly ground pepper
7. Take drained pasta and reserved liquid into a large bowl.
8. Add tomato mixture, asparagus. Add in grated cheese and toss well.
9. Serve with crusty bread and salad.

Boiled Ham with Mint Salsa

Ham cooked with vegetables and spices and served with mint salsa

Serves 4

Cooking time 25 minutes

Nutritional Information: Calories 312, Total Fat 4g, Protein 26g, Carbohydrates 46g, Dietary Fiber 8g

Ingredients

4 medium red potatoes, quartered

1 piece boneless fully cooked ham (16 ounces)

1/2 medium head cabbage, cut into wedges

6 medium carrots, halved lengthwise and cut into thirds

2 medium onions, cut into wedges

1/2 teaspoon whole allspice

1 teaspoon peppercorns

1 teaspoon dried thyme

1 garlic clove, halved

1 bay leaf

MINT SALSA

1 cup minced fresh mint

1/2 cup seeded chopped tomato

1 small cucumber, peeled, seeded and chopped

1/3 cup chopped sweet yellow pepper

1/3 cup finely chopped onion

1 jalapeno pepper, seeded and chopped

3 tablespoons lemon juice

3/4 teaspoon ground ginger

2 garlic cloves, minced

1/4 teaspoon salt

2 tablespoons sugar

Cooking Method

1. For mint salsa, mix all the ingredients in a bowl and refrigerate
2. Place the ham, potatoes, onions and carrots in a Dutch oven.
3. Add water just enough to cover the ham and vegetables
4. Join two cheesecloth and place peppercorns, bay leaf, garlic thyme and allspice on it.
5. Fold and tie the corners of cloth with a string.
6. Add this spice bag into the pan.
7. When the water starts boiling reduce heat; cover and simmer for 10 minutes.
8. Add cabbage; cover and simmer 15 minutes longer or until vegetables are tender
9. Discard spice bag. Serve with mint salsa

Skinny Fish with Cucumber Yoghurt Sauce

A mild-tasting, chunky-textured fish serves with potato chips and yoghurt sauce.

Serves 4

Cooking time 30 minutes

Nutritional Information: Calories 276, Total Fat 5g, Protein 27g, Carbohydrates 30g, Dietary Fiber2.8 g

Ingredients

1 1/2 pounds russet potatoes, cut in wedges

1 pound cod fillets, cut into four pieces

2 tsp olive oil

Pinch of Kosher salt

Juice and zest of 1 lemon

1/4 cup chopped parsley

Yoghurt Sauce

1/2 cup low fat Greek yogurt

3 tablespoons minced fresh parsley

1 large pickling cucumber, peeled, seeded, and diced

1 teaspoon fresh lemon juice

Cooking Method

1. Preheat oven to 425 degrees
2. To make yoghurt sauce; combine the parsley, yoghurt, salt, scallion, cucumber, lemon juice, and in a small bowl.
3. Cover potato wedges gently with oil and salt and arrange on a baking sheet.
4. Take another baking sheet and coat it with nonstick spray.
5. Place cod fillets on the sheet.
6. Squeeze lemon juice over fillets.
7. Place potatoes in preheated oven and cook for about 12 minutes.
8. Turn the potato wedges once and place again in the oven on a lower shelf.
9. Now place the fish on upper shelf of oven.
10. Roast for 12-15 minutes, until fish flakes easily with a fork.
11. Remove both potatoes and fish from the oven.
12. Sprinkle lemon zest and parsley on top of the fish.
13. Serve the fish with potato wedges and cucumber yoghurt sauce.

Conclusion

This is a book, full of easy low fat recipes for your favorite dishes that you thought you'd have to give up on a low fat eating plan. This book provides everything you'll ever need to know to produce delicious, energy-giving healthy food from the start of the day to last thing at night, from appetizers to full dinner parties; from meat specialities to vegetarian dishes of all kinds

These recipes are delicious and healthy and will help you lose weight for good. The recipes are very manageable and geared toward the average low fat cook who wants to feed their family healthier meals. Most of the recipes call for easy-to-find ingredients.

Whether you want to lose weight or maintain your already healthful weight, this book is all a foodie needs who know that healthy food should also mean delicious food.

Made in the USA
San Bernardino, CA
03 September 2016